Introduction

F OR 200,000 YEARS OF HUMAN LIFE ON EARTH, there was just one form of transport. It left a trail of footprints. In fact, the act of walking was one of the things that made the first people human. Our ancestors, the apes, could not walk (or run, or even stand) upright for long. Walking may have been slow, but using this first and simple form of transport, humans travelled from Africa, where they evolved, to far corners of Asia, Europe and America.

Would You Believe . . . ? Would You Believe . . . ? Would You Believe

Who, where, when and how?
Who wanted to stop the poor from taking trains? Where did postmen deliver ripe fruit to kings? When did special schools teach cycling? How do you make a ship from seaweed? Read on to find out the answers to these, and more, transport puzzles.

The invention of wheels, saddles and sails made transport easier and almost effortless, but it didn't get much faster. Until just two centuries ago, a ride on a galloping horse was the ultimate speed thrill. Then, with the arrival of railways, passengers could travel at the frightening speed of ... a car in a modern city's traffic.

Today, of course, we all take speed for granted. We think nothing of racing the sun half way across the world in aircraft. On the road, even the cheapest cars can accelerate to speeds that are dangerous and illegal. But we may be the last lucky generation to enjoy the luxury of speedy travel. As the fuel that we use to power our vehicles runs out, transport will surely slow down again. The wisest way to travel may, once more, be on our own two feet.

Transport
with Legs

Even ostriches can carry riders short distances.

TRAVELLING ON FOUR LEGS HAD A major advantage over a modern day car or bus: if you were really hungry at the end of a long journey, you could eat your transport! What we nowadays call saddle and pack (luggage) animals were actually first tamed for food some 5,500 years ago. People only began to use them for carrying heavy loads a lot later, at around the same time that they started harnessing various animals to very simple carts (see pages 8–9).

▼ **Mongol warriors**
Fast horses made the ancestors of these Mongol people from central Asia terrifying warriors. They swept across Europe in the 13th century, building an empire stretching from Austria to east China. When hungry, they opened up their horses' veins and drank their blood.

Without the Chinese invention of the stirrup, medieval knights could never have got into the saddle

The invention of the saddle with a tree (frame) in about 200 BCE made carrying loads easier for animals. A saddle spreads the weight of a rider over a wider area and gives the rider a safer seat. The Chinese fixed whole-foot stirrups to the saddle in the 4th century CE so riders could get on more easily and ride faster. There are now many styles of saddle. The western saddle was designed for cattle herders, who spent long hours on their horses.

Western saddle

Swift and strong, horses became the most valuable of all carrying beasts, ferrying conquering armies across Asia and Europe. However, horses needed a special diet and much care. In many places, hardy transport animals such as asses, onagers (wild asses), elephants and camels took their place.

Beasts of burden ▼
In many parts of the world, pack animals are still an important way of moving heavy loads. Camels, like this one from north Kenya, can travel great distances with very little water. Their wide feet do less damage to fragile landscapes than the tyres of motor vehicles.

Would You Believe . . . .?

Chinese postmen
Horse riders were no slouches. When 14th-century Venetian traveller Marco Polo visited China, he reported that messengers raced up to 800 km (500 miles) a day using relays of horses. As well as letters, they brought the emperor fresh fruit from distant, warmer regions.

5

Sleds, Skis
and Skates

S LIDING ON SNOW, slime and shiny ice is a slick way to travel. It's one of the very oldest, too. Many ancient peoples knew that dragging a heavy load was much easier than carrying it on their own backs. When the temperature dropped, travel got easier still, for even very heavy weights glide effortlessly along on slippery ice.

Special aids to ice sliding came from Scandinavia. Archaeologists have found 10,000-year-old sled runners in Finland. And rock drawings from 3000 BCE show Norwegians on skis. At this time, Finns skated between villages on frozen lakes.

Travois ▲
Native American peoples, such as these Assiniboin, moved their belongings on a two-legged skid-cart called a travois. Dogs pulled them until the 16th century, when European invaders introduced the much stronger horse.

Heavy loads ▼
Skids have been used to move heavy loads since ancient times. Egyptians used them to move the 3-tonne blocks of Khufu's Great Pyramid 20 centuries ago. This 19th-century log skidder allows two horses to move many times their own weight.

6

Would You Believe . . . ?

Horse-hoof men

People who first saw early skis called them "wooden horses". This led to the Greek myth of Hippododes – "men with horses' hooves". Chinese people of the T'ang dynasty (618–960) talked about "Turks who go hunting with wooden horses on their feet".

Survival **manuals** recommend the travois for emergency **transport of injured companions**

Mud slide ▶
Sliding transport still goes on where no other vehicle can reach. To bring his catch back across the slime of an English shoreline, shrimp fisherman Brendan Sellick uses a "mudhorse". Half barrow, half sledge, he leans on it and pushes it along with his feet.

Ski goddess ▶
Early Swedish writer Olaus Magnus was one of the first to describe a skier, in the 16th century: "...upon long stakes fastened to his feet he transported himself in a dangerous way by a winding motion". This Nordic ski goddess is an illustration in one of his books.

Winter games on the town moat by Esaias van de Velde

Skating for fun ▲
The first skates were made of bone. The Dutch then made iron ones, making skating easier and faster. By 1618, when this painting was done, people were using skates in sport as well as transport.

◀ **Modern snow-shoes**
Ordinary shoes sink into deep snow, making walking impossible. Strapping snow-shoes to the soles spreads the wearer's weight so they "float" on even the deepest drifts. Modern snow-shoes are made of light metal and plastic.

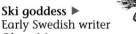

Modern hi-tech snow-shoes

Inventing the Wheel

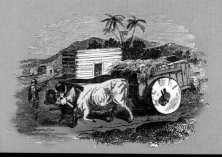

T HE MOST IMPORTANT TRANSPORT discovery was made by ... a potter! This was because wheels were first used under clay bowls in ancient Sumer (now Iraq). The first wheeled vehicles were probably created by fixing wheels to a sledge at least 5,500 years ago.

Wheels were such a new and amazing idea that at first they were an important sign of power: only kings would ride in carts. But as knowledge of the revolutionary invention spread, it changed first warfare and then every other kind of land transport.

Early wheel ▲
The very first wheels were not slices from logs, because these would have quickly split. Instead they were made from three separate planks of wood fastened together and cut to make a circular disc. Through a hole in the middle plank passed the axle – a thin rod around which the wheel could turn freely.

Chariots of war ▲
Pulled by onagers, and later horses, light chariots with spoked wheels were the terror weapons of the ancient world. Warriors swept down on their foes at speed and retreated as quickly. Chariots enabled the Hyksos people to conquer Egypt around 1630 BCE.

Golden chariot ▶
The ancient Egyptians improved the chariot by strengthening the wheels with more spokes and adding extra quivers (arrow-holders). This belt-buckle shows the pharaoh (god-king) Tutankhamun returning from battle in the 14th century BCE.

Wacky carriages

Drawn by horses, oxen and even elephants, wheeled vehicles made the transport of enormous cargoes over vast distances possible. Most were simple carts, wagons and carriages, but smart engineers also built special vehicles designed for speed or show.

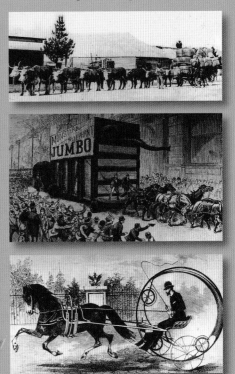

Chariot racing ▲
Roman people rode into battle on saddled horses, but chariot races at Rome's specially built track, the *Circus Maximus*, were wildly popular. As many as half a million came to cheer on their teams, which they supported like fans support football teams today. This poster depicts the chariot race in the stage production of *Ben-Hur*.

Would You Believe . . . . ?

Managing without wheels
Mexico's Aztec people put wheels on children's pull-along toys, but never used them on vehicles. This was probably because, until European invaders conquered Mexico in the 16th century, there were no pulling animals. People carried even the heaviest loads on their backs.

Goods, livestock and passengers ▲
Bullocks hauled this cart-load of wool in early 20th-century Australia (top). PT Barnum drew crowds in New York by showing the world's largest captive elephant in a special wagon (middle). Wheels spin inside wheels in the fast Polish *Swallow* of 1870 (bottom).

One wheel in China ▲
Chariots spread the wheel east to China. There, craft workers perfected it, making wheels with as many as 30 spokes. As well as creating multi-wheeled carts that carried enormous loads, they used single wheels to make wheelbarrows. Fitting sails to wheelbarrows allowed them to speed across China's flat, very windy plains.

One-wheeled Chinese "sailing carts" were built big enough to carry several passengers

9

Spinning Pedals

Would You Believe . . . ?

Riding schools
Learning to ride a velocipede (an early bike) was so hard that bike makers gave lessons in special riding halls. There, "velocipedagogues" taught cycling skills within a week. Though safer than on the roads, students emerged covered in cuts and bruises.

WITH SEATS as high as a man's shoulder, early bicycles needed very brave – or foolish – riders. Bumps in the road often caused fatal falls. So cyclists sighed with relief in the 1880s when these high-wheeled machines were replaced by bikes more like today's. They had two equal-sized wheels, pump-up tyres and a chain drive.

The new "safety bicycles" were a sensational success. They were the first personal transport that anyone could afford. Women riders, cycling in daring new clothes, tasted freedom, launching a movement for equality that still goes on.

Blooming women's lib ▲
Women could not cycle in long skirts, so they wore baggy pants beneath short skirts. The women's rights campaigner Amelia Bloomer made the loose pants very popular, and they were named "bloomers" after her.

◄ Bicycle ancestor
The first two-wheeled, human-powered vehicle was not a bike but the "running machine", or draisine. Named after its inventor, German baron Karl von Drais, it had no pedals. Riders used their feet to push it along. Briefly popular around 1820, it was then forgotten until the addition of pedals created the velocipede in the 1860s.

10

▲ Golden oldies
Cycling inspired inventors to make wildly original designs. Cycles with three and four wheels in uneven sizes were common, and multiple riders pedalled in peculiar positions.

Carbon wonder ▶
Today's fastest bikes are made of carbon fibre composites. However, though the materials have changed, the basic design is little different from the 1885 safety bicycle.

◀ Nursery toy
The body of this 19th-century hobby horse shows it's a toy, but in other ways it's similar to early tricycles. They too had bone-shaking wood frames and solid wheels with pedals attached.

Versatile vehicle ▼
Pedal-powered machines are still a useful form of transport. In places such as China, where roads are good but incomes are low, cycles transport goods, passengers and animals over short distances cheaply – and without pollution or fuel.

The very first bicycles came with optional sails so that the wind could give the rider a rest from pedalling

Iron Horse

THE INVENTION OF THE STEAM TRAIN in 1829 suddenly made travel at the terrifying speed of 24 kilometres (15 miles) an hour possible! A London professor, Dionysus Lardner, warned of the dangers: "passengers, unable to breathe, would die of asphyxia". They didn't of course, and the rails quickly spread across Europe and America.

Railways seemed to shrink the world: when tracks across the USA were completed in 1869, the journey from New York to San Francisco took just eight days. Previously, it had taken at least three months!

Goes like a rocket ▼
The railway revolution began in Britain. At an 1829 train race, the Rainhill Trials, the locomotive *Rocket* reached a top speed of 46 km/hr (29 mph). As well as cash, the feat won the loco the job of hauling train carriages on one of the first steam railways.

Shooting buffalo ▲
Railways did not always have a good effect. When trains crossed the North American plains, bored passengers passed the time by shooting rifles at buffalo grazing alongside the tracks. By 1900, these, as well as other hunts, had killed virtually all of the continent's 60 million buffalo.

Would You Believe . . . ?

Railway time
Until the railway age, each town set its clocks to different times. In Britain, St Ives in Cornwall, for example, was 20 minutes behind London because the sun rose 20 minutes later there. Train timetables forced everyone to set their clocks to the same time to avoid train crashes.

Fires, crashes and wrecks ▲
Nobody was badly hurt when this train left the rails and caught fire on New York's Brooklyn Bridge in 1903, but fatal accidents were fairly common from the earliest days of the railways. The very first passenger to die was British politician William Huskisson. The *Rocket* hit him at the opening of the Liverpool and Manchester Railway.

Travel for the poor
Rail travel was cheap, too. An 1844 law forced British railway companies to charge passengers no more than a penny a mile (1.6 km). Stagecoach fares were often eight times higher. For the first time, working people could afford to travel far away from their homes.

The King of Hanover said, "I do not wish every cobbler to be able to travel as quickly as I do."

Shinkansen bullet train ▲
Today, trains are by far the quickest way to travel on land. The fastest of all are the Japanese Shinkansen, or "bullet" trains. They speed along earthquake-proof tracks linking big cities at 300 km/hr (188 mph).

Buses, Subways
and Trams

ONLY THE SNOOTIEST PEOPLE were allowed on the first buses. The service, which ran in Paris in 1662, banned "soldiers, pages, lackeys, servants, workers and labourers". A really public bus started in the French city of Nantes in 1826. It was called an omnibus, a Latin word meaning "for all", to show it carried anyone.

Public buses ran on streets, but operators soon realised that the carriages rolled more easily on rails and they could double the passengers. Fifty people packed into each of New York's first horse-cars in 1852. Just two horses pulled these along rails.

Flogging a dead horse
Hungry and overworked, horses often dropped dead on the job, blocking already-crowded streets. To relieve jams, councils tried desperate remedies. They moved public transport beneath the ground, and up into the skies on "elevated railways".

Inside the subway ▲
When the first subway opened in London in 1863, steam trains that "bottled up their smoke" hauled carriages. The line built under New York's Broadway in 1870 (above), blew carriages along using air pressure. Electric power came 20 years later.

Horse-drawn omnibus ▼
The earliest bus service carried visitors from central Nantes to a nearby bath-house. The baths failed, but the bus service was very popular. It was copied first in Paris and then in many other cities, such as Glasgow (below). The buses gave a bumpy ride and were hardly quicker than walking.

ROYAL CALEDONIAN BASKET
GLASGOW & PAISLEY.

Keeping watch
When the New York subway opened in 1904, an astonished woman watched it for four days. Nicknamed "the sentinel" by employees, she sat on the platform at Times Square gasping, "Well! It's simply the greatest yet!" until her husband dragged her away.

Subway glamour

Underground transit systems were amazing achievements. Some were decorated like palaces to show their importance. Today, stainless steel has replaced marble, but cities are still proud of their ability to whiz millions to work each day.

El is for Elevated ▲
This propeller-driven railway is a 1924 fantasy. But in 1870, elevated railways did run high above the traffic in New York. The "El" were driven by electricity and cables. They were unpopular because breakdowns forced the passengers to descend to the ground on ladders.

◀ Shocking inventions
The first electric trams, which ran in Berlin in 1881, picked up power from the rails, which unfortunately also gave horses nasty shocks. Safer systems, such as overhead wires, made tram networks like this example from San Francisco popular until the mid 20th century.

Moscow metro ▲
The second-busiest city transport system after Tokyo, the Moscow metro is certainly the most ornate. The stations have chandeliers and patriotic scenes that aimed originally to inspire the communist workers who travelled the system daily.

They'll Frighten the Horses

BELCHING SMOKE AND SPARKS, the first motor cars looked like steam locomotives that had escaped from the track. They clanked noisily along on wheels rimmed with steel. No wonder they caused panic in city streets crowded with horse-drawn carriages.

The first of these clumsy cars ran in 1765 but they were hardly practical. "Horse power" meant real horses until the invention of petrol-driven cars more than a century later.

Cugnot's steam car ▲
French inventor Nicolas-Joseph Cugnot built the first motor vehicle around 1765. Weighing over two tonnes and driven by steam, it was designed to pull cannons. It wasn't a success: every 15 minutes the fire that powered it needed to be relit.

1888 Benz 1.5 horse power (hp) car

Petrol-driven ▲
The invention of the internal combustion engine made modern cars possible. Petrol burned inside these engines, driving the wheels of the cars they powered. This three-wheeler, made by German Karl Benz, was probably the first.

Douzième année. — Nº 572 Huit pages : CINQ centimes Dimanche 21 Janvier : 00.

Le Petit Parisien

TOUS LES JOURS
Le Petit Parisien
5 centimes.

SUPPLÉMENT LITTÉRAIRE ILLUSTRÉ
DIRECTION : 18, rue d'Enghien, PARIS

TOUS LES JEUDIS
SUPPLÉMENT LITTÉRAIRE
5 centimes.

CARREY

AUTOMOBILE ÉLECTRIQUE DES POMPIERS DE PARIS

◀ Batteries not included
When this French fire-engine raced to blazing buildings in 1900, electric vehicles were already 60 years old. In the early 20th century, electric cars sold better than petrol-powered models, but the need to recharge them made them inconvenient.

Red flag ▶
Early British motor cars were treated like trains. They had to have three people with them, one of whom walked 55 m (180 ft) ahead waving a red flag. Until the law was relaxed in 1896, cars could only travel at walking pace.

Costly cars
Even when "horseless carriages" became more common, they were still luxuries. The smallest cost 18 months' wages for many workers. Motoring was a dream for most until Ford pioneered cheap vehicles.

Model T Ford ▲
In 1908, American inventor Henry Ford cut the cost of making cars by using standard parts and by having each worker do one bit of the whole job. His Model T moved along a "production line" as workers added parts. He paid his staff so well that they could afford cars themselves.

Would You Believe...?

The motor cow
Not all engineers wanted cars to have wheels. Many thought wheels would spin uselessly and instead invented four-legged walking machines. American John Pratt, for example, designed a vehicle in 1879 that "simulated the movement of the hind legs of a cow".

In 1899 the *Literary Digest* reported that "The horseless carriage is a luxury. It will never come into common use."

Motor Cars
and Traffic Jams

A view of pollution due to the steam car

A S EXHAUST FUMES CHOKE OUR cities, it's easy to forget that the first motor cars were seen as a cure for pollution, not a cause. The horse-drawn transport they replaced left the city streets covered in stinking dung. Cars were thought to be the cleaner alternative!

Cars offered a dream of personal freedom. Drivers could travel everywhere and live anywhere. But by the late 20th century, the dream was becoming a nightmare. Cars clogged roads and – through climate change – their fumes threatened life itself.

Would You Believe . . . ?

That's progress?
Traffic jams have slowed motorists everywhere, but Londoners have the slowest moving traffic in Europe. At 19 km/hr (12 mph), cars move through the streets of Britain's capital no faster than the horses and carts that they replaced a century ago.

Fins and chrome ▶

By the mid 20th century, motor cars had become much more than just a way to get around. After houses, they were the most expensive things that anyone bought, and motorists used them to display their wealth and good taste. Shiny chrome and huge fins suggested speed and glamour. The 1959 Cadillac Coupe de Ville was the most extravagant example of this. Styled like a jet aircraft, it was nearly 6 m (19 ft) long.

▲ Paris gridlock

Today, all major cities have traffic problems. Motor cars that once liberated people now imprison them. City councils struggle to control jams by improving public transport, charging cars to enter or – as in Paris – providing free bikes.

▲ Changing landscape

No country was more affected by the growth of motor transport than the USA. Cars, and the speedy movement they gave, allowed people to live far from their work. Weak planning controls let suburbs of houses spread, and green fields disappeared under sprawling roads.

● ● ● ● ● ● ● ● ● ● ● ● ● ● ● ●

Motorists spend a quarter of their time in jams, yet they still prefer their cars to public transport

◀ Cars and horses

This 1914 photo of London's Piccadilly Circus would be very different to the same scene 20 years before. Motor buses had replaced horse-drawn buses in just ten years, and there were already more motor taxis than horse-drawn cabs.

Future cars ▶

Gas-guzzling cars are too big and wasteful for the 21st century. The future lies in tiny, economical cars like the battery-powered Tango. More like a motor bike than a car, it fits into a quarter of a normal parking space.

Wet and Wild
Journeys

◀ A Tibetan skin boat

NEED TO CROSS A river? Try this. Slaughter the nearest beast, carefully remove its skin, tie up the neck and all other holes, fill with air and float across. Do you think this sounds far-fetched? Think again! Some of the very first water travellers probably sat on these inflated skin floats.

However, skin floats aren't boats, and easily turn over. To avoid a drenching, primitive mariners soon found better ways of crossing water. They stretched skin over a frame, lashed together bundles of reeds or turned a tree into a craft.

Skin coracles ▲
Stretched over a wooden frame, animal skin makes a buoyant boat that's light enough to carry around rapids. Skin craft were used by the Mandan people on North America's Missouri river, but they were also used as far away as Wales and India.

Pacific war canoe ▼
New Zealand's Maori people were expert boat builders. They made huge war canoes that carried as many as 140 warriors. Called waka, these boats were up to 80 m (262 ft) long and elaborately carved. They were kept upright with double hulls or outriggers (floats).

Nile reed boat
Some 6,000 years ago, ancient Egyptians were making simple boats from the reeds that lined the Nile river. Tied in bundles, the reeds could be made into everything from a hunting float like a surfboard, to a ship fit for a king.

Dugout canoe ▼
Many ancient peoples hollowed out trees to make dugout canoes. They set fires on a log and then scraped out the charcoal with stone blades. This example is from Papua New Guinea.

Paddle power

Boats skimmed rivers and lakes half a million years ago. They floated downstream, their passengers pushing them along using hands or paddles. For longer distances, they depended on the winds, tides and currents. In such simple craft, some people made dangerous journeys across the oceans.

Birch bark boat ▲
Stripping the bark quickly turns a tree into a lightweight water craft like this canoe built by North America's Ojibwe people. The bark is soft and flexible when fresh-cut, but sets hard as it dries. Seams are sewn tight shut and a coat of tree gum seals any holes.

Would You Believe . . . ?

Monster barges
Egyptian shipwrights made the world's biggest ships in the 16th century BCE to carry stone down the Nile. A barge the length of a football pitch and weighing 7,300 tonnes was built to carry an obelisk (stone column). No bigger ship was built for 3,000 years.

Masts
and Yards

ROWING AND PADDLING IS hard work, but with the wind behind them, sailors can rest and get blown along. Some 5,000 years ago, an Egyptian mariner had a brilliant idea. He raised a sheet of canvas up high to catch more of the breeze. The sail that he created transformed transport.

◀ **Christopher Columbus**
In 1492, Italian-Spanish explorer Columbus was the first European to sail across the Atlantic to the "new lands". His crew feared travelling to an unknown continent, so he lured four criminals on board with the offer of freedom if they joined.

Nile sailing ▲
In ancient Egypt, ships drifted north with the current down the Nile. Crews rowed upstream until they found that a sail would take them, because Egypt's winds blow south.

Sailing was fast. With a good wind behind them, ships could travel as far as 750 km (470 miles) a day. Sailing ships made it possible for Europeans to reach the most distant oceans quickly and conquer the lands on their shores.

◀ **Not a load of junk**
Chinese sailing ships were far in advance of those from Europe, and far bigger. Nearly a century before Columbus crossed the Atlantic in the 26 m (85 ft) *Santa Maria*, Chinese mariners were sailing to Africa in junks four times as big.

Sailing

Nothing could beat sailing for speed until the mid 19th century (see pages 24–25). Since then, slick sailing ships have raced across the world's waters mostly for sport and pleasure. In the future, though, sail may once again conquer the oceans as oil becomes scarce and costly.

Square rigger ▶
Northern European ocean-sailing ships carried sails rigged (hanging) from beams called yards. They hung square (across the hull). This square rig was powerful but needed large crews.

Modern sails ▲
Triangular sails running along the hull were invented by Mediterranean sailors. Today, most sailing ships carry this fore-and-aft rig. It gives them speed, and they don't need big crews because there are only a few sails to handle.

Skysails ▲
Giant kites may soon make sailing cargo ships popular once again. Launched under computer control, the kites tow along vessels such as the *MS Beluga Skysails*, saving up to one-third of the fuel the ships would otherwise consume.

Salt-caked Smokestacks

PUFFING, SNORTING AND BELCHING smoke, the first steamships were like dirty smudges in harbours filled with white sails. Few believed they would last, until 1807, when a steamboat began carrying passengers regularly on the Hudson river in New York. Less than a century later, sailing ships would look like antiques.

Mississippi steamer ▲
Some of the very first steamboats were on the Mississippi river in the USA. From 1811, they carried timber, coal, cotton, and passengers from St Louis to New Orleans. Many were ornate, with several decks and tall funnels.

Early paddle steamers stuck to rivers and lakes because they often had to stop for coal for their engines. Another problem was that ocean swell lifted the two paddle wheels in turn from the water, which meant the ship zig-zagged along. Screws (propellers) later solved this problem.

The end of an era ▼
By the time the Brooklyn Bridge was completed in 1883, steamships outnumbered sailing ships in New York's most famous harbour. They tied up at the huge wharves that lined Manhattan Island's shores on the East and Hudson rivers.

Would You Believe . . . ?

Riverboat writer
Working as a riverboat pilot from 1857, Samuel Clemens listened for the lookout's shout of "mark twain!" signalling deep water. When Sam gave up his piloting job to write books such as *Huckleberry Finn*, he borrowed the phrase to use as his pen name.

Crossing the oceans

Ocean travel seemed impossible for steamers. But, on 23 April 1838, a gigantic paddle steamer arrived in New York just 15 days after leaving England. The SS *Great Western* had sails, but these were used mainly to keep the ship upright so that both of the paddle wheels stayed in the water.

Conquering the Atlantic ▲

The SS *Great Western* was designed by Isambard Brunel, chief engineer of Britain's Great Western Railway Company. He jokingly named the ship to suggest that it was extending railway lines across the Atlantic.

Powering giants ▶

Spinning deep beneath the water, propellers drove ships more efficiently than paddle wheels and needed less-complicated machinery in the engine room. These colossal propellers were driving the Atlantic liner *Titanic* when she hit an iceberg and sank in 1912.

◀ 1848 tug-of-war

When paddle steamers ruled the waves, propellers were a novelty – until the British navy staged a tug-of-war between the propeller-powered *Rattler* and paddle steamer *Alecto*. They had similar engines but *Rattler* won, towing *Alecto* backwards.

● ● ● ● ● ● ● ● ● ● ● ● ●

Today, most of what we buy from abroad, from fuel oil to toys, is delivered by truly vast steamships. The biggest cargo ship, *Emma Maersk*, is 400 m (1,300 ft) long. Even the huge SS *Great Western* would fit easily on her deck – 15 times over!

▲ Barges today

A barge is six times more fuel-efficient than a lorry. Rivers and canals that were neglected in the 20th century may once more provide a green way to transport heavy and bulky freight. This barge is on the Danube in Hungary.

Floating
Cities

The truth about emigration ▲ ▼
In the late 19th century, many millions of emigrants crossed the Atlantic on ocean liners in big "steerage" class cabins. These were often hot, crowded, airless and filthy, and always in the worst part of the ship. Publicity posters painted a much more pleasant picture (below).

ENORMOUS! COLOSSAL! Humongous! There just aren't words big enough to describe the monster passenger ships we call ocean liners. These vast craft were first built to ferry migrants from Europe to America.

When emigration slowed down in the 1920s, shipping companies tried to reinvent the liner. They built faster, grander ships, and created floating cities, aiming to give wealthy passengers every luxury they enjoyed ashore.

▼ Doomed monster
When the RMS (Royal Mail Ship) *Titanic* (below) was launched in 1911, it was the most advanced liner afloat. However, the ship struck an iceberg and sunk on its first voyage. Wealthy travellers crowded the few lifeboats, and most of the crew and 3rd-class passengers drowned.

Independence of the Seas ▼ ▶
Longer than three soccer pitches, the huge 15-deck *Independence of the Seas* is one of the largest cruise ships afloat. More than 4,000 passengers can enjoy facilities like an ice rink, a surfing pool and a shopping street.

Liners today

In the 1950s, ocean liners lost their richest passengers after jet aircraft made flying fast and popular. Many ships were scrapped. Some became cruise liners. Today, a new generation of liners is planned. Bigger than anything before, their vast cabins will be floating apartments for the super-rich.

● ● ● ● ● ● ● ● ● ● ● ● ●

The RMS *Titanic*'s gymnasium had a mechanical camel that passengers rode for exercise

Lighter than Air

◄ **Montgolfier balloon**
The Montgolfier brothers, Joseph-Michel and Jacques-Étienne didn't join the first crewed balloon flight. Instead, François Laurent d'Arlandes and Jean-François Pilatre de Rozier soared above Paris, in 1783.

WATCHING burning paper float up from their fire, two French brothers had a brilliant idea. They opened a paper bag above the embers of the fire. As it filled with smoke and rose up the chimney, the brothers realised a big enough bag could lift passengers into the air.

The Montgolfier brothers lost no time and made the first transport balloon. In 1783, it carried aloft a chicken, a duck and a sheep called Climb-to-the-sky.

MORT DE HARRIS (1824)

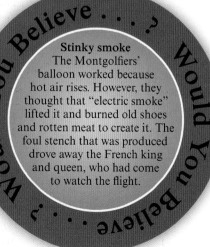

Would You Believe . . . ?

Stinky smoke
The Montgolfiers' balloon worked because hot air rises. However, they thought that "electric smoke" lifted it and burned old shoes and rotten meat to create it. The foul stench that was produced drove away the French king and queen, who had come to watch the flight.

Terrible dangers
The Montgolfiers' balloon inspired others. The worried French king insisted balloons carry only criminals. He was persuaded to let volunteers try to fly, but many flights ended in disaster.

Heroes or fools? ▲
Ballooning accidents were common. Thomas Harris (above) died in 1824 when the gas valve jammed. As the balloon lost height, he jumped to his death to lighten the basket and save his fiancé.

Copper balloons
A century before the Montgolfiers, Italian priest Francesco Lana de Terzi suggested sucking the air out of four large copper balls and fixing them to a boat. He believed – mistakenly – that the balls would be so light that they would float up into the air.

◄▲ All shapes and sizes
Today, hot-air balloons – some in novelty shapes – are used mostly for sport. The biggest provide the ultimate joy-ride. Lifted with helium gas and hot air, the 55-m (180-ft)-high *Breitling Orbiter 3* was the first balloon to go round the world, in 1999.

▲ Aeroscraft ML866
By combining lighter-than-air lifting gas with a specially shaped hull, this modern air vehicle is neither balloon nor aeroplane. It can hover and rise straight up from the ground, so it can take off and land almost anywhere. There is a passenger and freight version of the craft.

The development of balloons continued, and on 1 December 1783 a balloon filled with hydrogen lifted two scientists 600 m (2,000 ft) into the sky. At last humans could join the birds.

Flaming ► disaster
Balloon travel came to a halt in 1937 when the airship (powered balloon) *Hindenburg* crashed on landing in New Jersey, USA. Filled with flammable hydrogen, it burned fiercely. Helium gas used in today's balloons is safe because it doesn't burn.

When the first balloon drifted to earth, French villagers thought it was a monster and tore it to bits

Getting it Wright

Greek flapper ▲
People had dreamed of flying since ancient times. A Greek myth tells how Icarus and his father Daedalus built wax and feather wings to escape from prison. Icarus flew too close to the sun. The wax melted and he fell to his death. This painting by Merry-Joseph Blondel is on a ceiling of the Louvre museum in Paris.

OST "BIRD men" were just jokes in 1896. Strapping various designs of wings to their backs, they jumped from hills and towers and tried to flap into the air. Few took off and fewer flew. However, two American bicycle mechanics, Wilbur and Orville Wright, weren't laughing. They were sure they could build flying machines.

German bird man ▲
One bird man really did fly. German Otto Lilienthal made more than ten bat-wing craft, a bit like hang-gliders, and flew up to 350 m (1,150 ft). But in 1896, a gust of wind upset his balance and he fell to his death.

- The Wright brothers were amateurs. They had famous and wealthy competitors. But they tackled the problem of flight scientifically. When their wings didn't soar as high as they expected, they tested them out – on a bike. They strapped a section of wing to the handlebars and pedalled furiously to simulate the rush of air that lifted their craft.

Glider flown as a kite 1900   Glider flown as a kite 1901   Wilbur gliding 1901

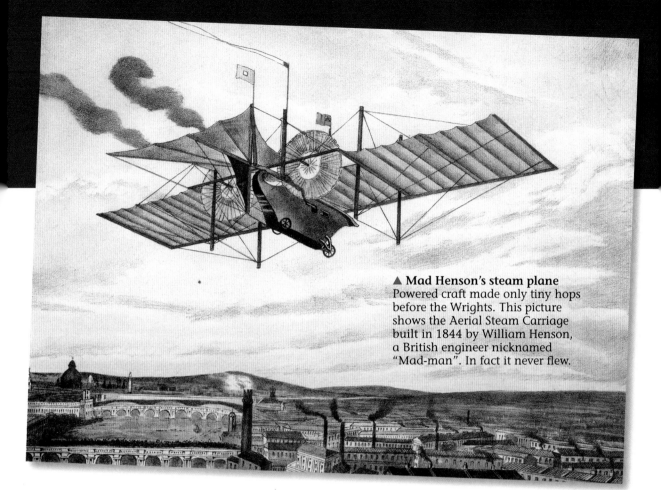

▲ **Mad Henson's steam plane**
Powered craft made only tiny hops
before the Wrights. This picture
shows the Aerial Steam Carriage
built in 1844 by William Henson,
a British engineer nicknamed
"Mad-man". In fact it never flew.

Flight in pictures

Wilbur and Orville were keen
photographers and carefully
recorded their achievements.
Below are some of their black-
and-white slides. Their first flying
machines were like giant kites.
They took it in turns to ride
them on windy beaches. Bending
the wings controlled direction.

First flight ▼
By 1903, the Wright brothers were ready. They returned
to windy Kill Devil Hills, South Carolina, where they had
flown gliders for three autumns. This time they had a new
craft, propellers and a home-made, lightweight engine.
There, a week before Christmas, Orville soared into the air
on the world's first powered flying machine, the *Flyer*.

A fixed tail 1902   Start of a glide 1902

First powered flight 17 December 1903

Flying Grows Up

WILBUR AND ORVILLE WRIGHT showed the world that flight was actually possible, though you wouldn't have wanted to travel on their *Flyer*. The pilot lay on the wing! The first record-making flight was less than half the length of a modern jumbo jet. But once the Wrights had shown the way, everybody wanted to fly.

Rich adventurers and dare-devils were the first to take to the air. They raced planes and risked their lives to break records. But war broke out in 1914 and then aviation became deadly serious. Pilots fought bravely in the dangerous skies above Europe's battlefields.

Flight for all

After the war, aircraft became safer, faster and more comfortable. Metal replaced canvas skins and wood-and-wire frames. Jet engines made vast, fast aircraft possible. And flight, once a glamorous adventure, became a tedious ordeal!

Louis Blériot ▼
Usually accident-prone French pilot Louis Blériot amazed the world in 1909 when he flew across the Channel from France to England, scooping a £1,000 prize from the *Daily Mail*. The paper announced the flight with the headline "England is no longer an island".

Would You Believe . . . ?

Fasten seat belts
Passengers had a hard time in 1930s aircraft. Although food was served on china plates, the cabin was so noisy and cold that people had to wear earplugs and heavy coats, and the lavatory was just a draughty seat above a hole in the fuselage.

Scary war plane ▶
World War I fighter planes could be scary to fly. The British Sopwith Camel, for example, was better at turning right than left. Pilots joked that flying one would win them a Victoria Cross (bravery medal) or a wooden cross (battlefield grave).

IMPERIAL AIRWAYS
AND ASSOCIATED COMPANIES

◀ ▼ Passenger travel
At first, flying was only for the very wealthiest passengers. In 1935, when Imperial Airways opened their London-to-Australia route, a one-way ticket cost 70 weeks' wages for an average worker. Flying on the first jets, introduced in 1950, was so glamorous that passengers were called the "jet set". Cheap flights arrived in the 1970s when jumbo jets cut costs.

10½ DAYS

The Airbus 380 seats 850 people on two floors.

Whirlybirds
Like the Wrights, helicopter inventor Paul Cornu was a bike mechanic. His 1907 craft hovered but was impossible to control. It wasn't until the 1940s that helicopters were practical. "Choppers" are still noisy, slow and expensive to fly – but nevertheless essential.

Copters at work ▲
The ability to hover on the spot and land in difficult places, such as on a flat rooftop, makes helicopters invaluable to many people. They can help out wherever there is no space to operate a regular plane, such as in firefighting (top) and as sky-cranes (bottom).

A Sound Idea

IN 1947, HIGH ABOVE CALIFORNIA'S Mojave Desert, a pilot radioed his engineer from a secret plane: the X-1. "There's something wrong with this machmeter ... it's gone kinda screwy on me." With this message, Chuck Yeager revealed he had flown faster than sound.

Reaching the speed of sound was a sensational achievement. Engineers feared aircraft would crash if they flew faster than sound – 1,240 km/hr (770 mph) or "Mach 1".

▲ Noisy barrier
Trailing behind a supersonic (faster-than-sound) aircraft is a shock wave. It's sometimes visible as the mist-like cone shown here. More obvious is its sound – a loud "sonic boom".

Super fighter ▼
Eight years after Yeager's flight, the F-100 Super Sabre became the first supersonic fighter. Today, all fighters fly faster than Mach 2 (twice sound's speed).

Rocking rocket ▼
Chuck Yeager became a hero after his flight in the X-1, which he nicknamed Glamorous Glennis after his wife. A bomber lifted him to 8 km (5 miles). On release, the X-1 fired a rocket, which blasted it to record speeds.

GLAMOROUS GLENNIS

Flying a legend ▲ ▶
In *Concorde's* cockpit, the machmeter
(speedometer) is just below the left leg of the
M-shaped control stick on the right. At full
speed, *Concorde* reached Mach 2.02. It
could cross the Atlantic in just three and
a half hours, but passengers paid a high
price for the speed – up to 60 times a
tourist class fare in ordinary planes.

Supersonic speed heated *Concorde's* skin so much that the aircraft expanded by 30 cm (1 ft) in flight

Some called the speed of sound the "sound barrier",
because as aircraft approached this speed, they shook
and flight controls no longer worked. But the X-1
rocket plane showed that the barrier could be broken.

Speed kings
Fighter pilots soon regularly flew as fast as Yeager. Ordinary
passengers had to wait until *Concorde*, a supersonic airliner,
flew. Though fast and sleek, *Concorde* was costly, polluting and
so noisy that it flew at full speed only over empty oceans.

Wild Blue Yonder

▼ Space fiction
French author Jules Verne wrote *De la Terre à la Lune* (*From the Earth to the Moon*) in 1865. He imagined cannons blasting craft skywards. In reality, such a launch would crush those on board.

FOR TRANSPORT enthusiasts, the ultimate trip is out of this world. People have dreamed of soaring free of the Earth's gravity since our ancestors first gazed up at the Moon. However, crewed space vehicles only became a reality half a century ago. After the first historic Earth orbit, the USA and Russia began to race each other all the way to the Moon.

The USA won the race, landing a bug-like craft on the Moon's surface in summer 1969. More distant targets are still out of reach, but this hasn't slowed space exploration.

JULES VERNE

DE LA TERRE À LA LUNE
autour de la Lune

VOYAGES EXTRAORDINAIRES
Collection Hetzel

Would You Believe . . . ?

Moist Moon walk
When *Apollo 11* lunar module pilot Buzz Aldrin stepped out on to the Moon, he was so excited by the experience that he peed in his space suit. Fortunately, mission engineers had prepared for everything: space suits had collection bottles for just such mishaps.

The real future of space travel

Since the *Apollo* missions ended in 1975, crewed craft haven't left Earth's orbit. Their pilot and scientist passengers are now being joined by a new kind of astronaut: tourists. Thrill seekers are already queuing to pay US $200,000 for flights to the edge of space.

▲ First spaceman
Russian Yuri Gagarin became the first cosmonaut (space traveller) when he orbited Earth on 12 April, 1961. On his return to Earth, Gagarin left his *Vostok 1* capsule 7 km (23,000 ft) above the ground and descended by parachute. This was kept secret for fear that the spaceman's envious American rivals might challenge his record because he did not land inside his craft.

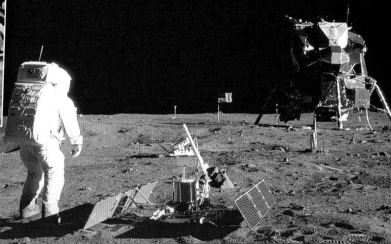

▲ Footsteps on the Moon
Humiliated by Gagarin's flight, American leaders vowed to land men on the Moon. Eight years later, the *Apollo 11* mission achieved that goal. Here, mission commander Neil Armstrong runs experiments near the craft in which he and Buzz Aldrin landed.

SpaceShipOne attached under its mothership *White Knight*

▲ Piggy-back ride to space
Tomorrow's space tourists won't be hearing "3-2-1 BLAST OFF!" Instead they will ride in a capsule slung beneath a small aircraft. At 16 km (52,000 ft), the capsule will fall away then fire its rocket motor to blast it to 100 km (60 miles) above the Earth and a six-minute weightless space flight. *SpaceShipOne* is a test craft that pioneered "piggy-back" space flights.

The rocket on *SpaceShipOne* is powered by rubber and nitrous oxide – the "laughing gas" once used by dentists

Is it a Boat or a Plane?

AT FIRST glance, transport seems simple. Floating, rolling and flying get us about on water, land and air. But look closely, and things become more complicated. What about vehicles that travel on land and sea? Or both water and air? Inventors love in-between-craft, like the cyclo-boat above.

▼ **Orukter Amphibolos**

American inventor Oliver Evans built this amphibious vehicle in 1805 to dig mud from Philadelphia's dockyards. Driven by wheels and paddles, it was not a success, but the steam engine he invented to drive it, was, later powering Mississippi steamers.

Hydrofoil ▲

Beneath the hull of a hydrofoil are stubby wings shaped like those on an aircraft. Instead of air, water flows over the wings to lift the craft above the waves as it picks up speed. Hydrofoils like this one provide a fast "bus service" between Greece's many islands in the Aegean and Mediterranean seas.

Some of these versatile vehicles really work. They are especially valuable in the "not-sure" worlds where land and water meet in messy mud or ice. Or where travellers have to move quickly from land to sea – and then back again.

Flying – but only just

There are a few different kinds of boat that fly. Hovercraft, the best known surface-skimming vehicles, ride on air cushions. Hydrofoils ride on an underwater wing and ekranoplanes (right) fly in a similar way to aircraft, although they never rise more than a few metres into the air!

▲ A Soviet ekranoplane from the 1980s, the world's heaviest aircraft.

US spy satellites spotted the Soviet ekranoplanes, and they were nicknamed "Caspian Sea Monsters"

Frog craft

Amphibious vehicles are named after amphibians, such as frogs and newts, which are equally at home on land and in ponds. There are cars that float, but these are happiest on land, and boats with wheels, which work best in water.

Would You Believe . . . ?

Cunning invention
British hovercraft inventor Christopher Cockerell used a hairdryer and two tin cans to prove his idea worked. Nesting the tins one inside the other and directing air through the gap between them produced more lifting power than a direct blast on one can on its own.

◄ **Hovercraft**
Giant fans create a cushion of air beneath the flexible "skirt" of a hovercraft, lifting it off the ground or sea. Because the air cushion presses gently down, hovercraft can operate on soft surfaces like mud, which are barriers to boats and wheeled vehicles.

Versatile vehicles ▲
Rinspeed's sQuba car (top) really does drive underwater, but its open top makes wetsuits essential. An amphibious bus (middle) is a novel way for tourists to see sights from land and water. And this German police car (bottom) can follow villains wherever they flee.

Setting the Record

High flyer ▶
Sometimes the slowest competitor takes the record. NASA's 2001 *Helios* "flying wing" travelled at 40 km/hr (25 mph) but soared to a record 30 km (18 miles) high. The 14 motors that turned the propellers were powered by solar panels, so night flights were a problem!

Zeppelin train ▼
Built in Germany in 1930, the Rail Zeppelin set a world railway speed record of 230 km/hr (140 mph) that was unbeaten for 23 years. The large wooden propeller fitted to the train's rear car alarmed people on platforms that it passed.

PIONEERING PROJECTS OR JUST pointless pranks? Breaking transport records can be either of these. Record enthusiasts claim that their costly, clever vehicles push technology forwards. But nobody denies that record chasing is dangerous: drivers, pilots and even spectators have taken terrible and fatal risks.

The danger, of course, is part of the thrill. When cars raced at Staten Island, New York, in 1902, spectators gathered at the most hazardous spot. Many paid highly for their grisly curiosity: a car left the track and ploughed into the crowd.

The Rail Zeppelin travelled faster than a passenger plane of the time.

Road tests

Today's bullet-fast cars break records on deserted tracks, but cars once raced on public roads. In 1901, residents of Newport, USA, complained that races of 100 km/hr (60 mph) were "a menace to life". British road racers obeyed speed limits of 20 km/hr (12 mph)!

Speedy boat ▲

In 2008, the *Earthrace* trimaran broke the round-the-world powerboat record, taking just 61 days. The boat uses "green" biofuel, but if food crops were planted on the land used to grow the fuel, they would feed 1,600 children for a year.

Record benefits

Today's speed attempts are far safer than in the past. It's technology, not reckless risk, that breaks records. Some race technology even finds its way into ordinary road vehicles. For example, new cars are made fuel-efficient using wind-tunnel tests, a technique that was once used only for exotic racers.

Hero and zero ▲ ▶

With the world's smallest diesel engine, the Smart Fortwo cdi (above) also holds the record for low CO_2 emissions. As a contrast, the Bugatti Veyron (right) is the world's fastest accelerating road car – and it uses eight times more fuel than the Smart car.

◀ **At €1.1 million, the Bugatti Veyron is one of the most costly cars.**

◀ **Diesel racer**

Two souped-up JCB digger engines power this sleek yellow racer. The JCB Dieselmax set a world speed record for a diesel-engined vehicle in 2006, speeding to an impressive 560 km/hr (350 mph) on Bonneville Salt Flats – a dry lake in Utah, USA.

Fantasy or Invention?

Skycar
Because they take off and land vertically, Moller Skycars don't need a landing strip. Little bigger than SUVs (sports utility vehicles), they are five times as fast and use the same amount of fuel. Skycars aren't for sale yet, and they'd be the ultimate noisy-neighbour nuisance.

HUMAN BEINGS ARE endlessly restless and inventive, so it's hardly surprising that they are constantly seeking easier, faster or fun new ways to get around. Some ideas are fairly sensible, some seem downright suicidal and some are quite simply science fiction.

Few new inventions succeed. Huge sums have been spent on roads, railways and airports, so to compete with vehicles that use these, anything new must be amazing.

Would You Believe . . . ?

Straight up at the lights
Flying cars are not a new idea. Motor tycoon Henry Ford built one in 1926, predicting, "A combination airplane and motor car is coming. You may smile. But it will come." However, when a crash killed his test pilot, Ford stopped the project.

Flying saucers
Fact and fiction blurred in the 1950s when the US army and air force secretly developed the Avrocar. Shaped like a flying saucer, it was invented by Canadian Jack Frost. It was supposed to hover then soar like a fighter aircraft. Two were built, but pilots found them too hard to fly.

Keeping it personal

Inventors keep dreaming. Most of their fantasies involve making transport personal. Segway scooters provide a solitary ride. Jet packs make their individual pilots as free as birds. And the appeal of personal aircraft is obvious to anyone who hates public transport.

◀ **Personal Transporter**
The Segway PT is an electric, self-balancing platform that goes as fast as an Olympic sprinter. The rider brakes, accelerates and steers by leaning backwards, forwards and sideways. Here, German police are riding them.

Jet packs ▲ ▶
Spacewalking astronauts wear emergency jet packs (above) which can propel them back to the capsule if their tether snaps. Jet packs for use on Earth (right) must be far more powerful to balance gravity. So far, only plucky inventors have flown them.

Segway riders in San Francisco's Bay Area meet to play polo, with the same mallets, balls and rules as the horsey sport

The Batbike ▼
Unlike many Hollywood props, the Batbike actually works! Built for the 2008 movie *The Dark Knight*, it has engines inside each wheel. The cannons and machine guns are just for show!

Science fact or fiction?

So what actually separates real vehicles from fantasy ones? Very little, in fact! The Avrocars built secretly for America's spies were real-life flying saucers. And the Batbike, a pure Hollywood dream, is steered not with the hands but with the shoulders – very like a Segway scooter.

What will there be in the Future?

PREDICTING THE FUTURE OF transport is as risky as jumping a red light: you never know what's around the corner. Only one thing's for sure. Ingenious inventors will continue to seek clever solutions to transport problems. They are going to be very busy.

Getting about will soon be a lot more difficult. The oil that powers most vehicles is fast running out. Electric cars are no answer: most electric power is generated by burning oil or gas. Nor are biofuels: they compete for land with food crops.

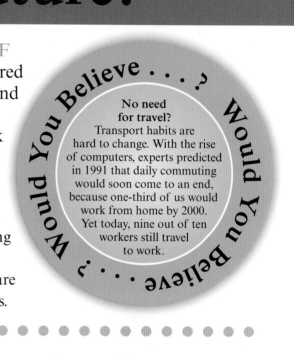

Would You Believe . . . ? Would You Believe . . . ?

No need for travel? Transport habits are hard to change. With the rise of computers, experts predicted in 1991 that daily commuting would soon come to an end, because one-third of us would work from home by 2000. Yet today, nine out of ten workers still travel to work.

Our warming world

There's another problem too. Burning oil has changed the Earth's climate. If we all drive fast, thirsty cars, our children will roast in a greenhouse world. So, soon, very soon, the luxury of family cars, which we have enjoyed for the last century, must end. The future is public transport.

◄ **Hi-tech wonder or climate folly?**
Armadillo Aerospace is one of many companies planning tourist space flights. Their Pixel vertical-take-off vehicle, shown here, won a 2008 NASA prize for hovering as if on the Moon's surface. Projects like these are exciting, but can we afford them? Fuelling just today's cars and planes is making our fragile planet impossible to live on.

Together, climate change and rising fuel prices will soon make flying a luxury only the super-rich can afford

Find out More

You can find out lots more about the history of transport from these websites and places to visit.

Websites

Steam Machine
www.pbs.org/wgbh/nova/monitor/engine2.html
Stoke the engine, open the valves and watch the wheels turn on the engine that powered a US Civil War battleship. Mind it doesn't explode.

Fly left to Wright
www.pbs.org/wgbh/nova/wright
Explore this website for stacks of information about the Wright brothers and some great games.

Get me out of here
www.nms.ac.uk/planebuilder.aspx
Build a plane that will fly you safely home in this game from the National Museum of Scotland website.

Iceberg alert
www.titanicinbelfast.com/learnmore.aspx
Learn about shipbuilding on this site about the *Titanic*. It includes a section on keeping it afloat!

Messing about in boats
www.motorboatmuseum.org.uk/learning/games.php
You may sink the boat but you won't get wet playing these great games on the Motorboat Museum's site.

Places to visit

National Railway Museum
Leeman Road, York YO26 4XJ
Telephone: 08448 153139
Website: www.nrm.org.uk
Over 100 locomotives, including a replica of Stephenson's *Rocket* and the Japanese Bullet Train, tell the railway story from the early 19th century to the present day.

London Transport Museum
Covent Garden Piazza, London WC2E 7BB
Telephone: 020 7379 6344
Website: www.ltmuseum.co.uk
Find out about everything to do with transport in London. There's loads to see and explore.

The Science Museum
Exhibition Road, London SW7 2DD
Telephone: 0870 780 9486
Website: www.sciencemuseum.org.uk
Trains, boats and planes – they're all here, from steam power to space flights. It has the *real* Stephenson's *Rocket*.

Museum of Transport
1 Bunhouse Road, Glasgow G3 8DP
Telephone: 0141 287 2720
Website: www.glasgowmuseums.com/venue/index.cfm?venueid=7
The story of Scottish transport, including a celebration of the Clyde shipbuilding industry. See the Glasgow trams or visit the "Subway" station.

Coventry Transport Museum
Millennium Place, Hales Street, Coventry CV1 1PN
Telephone: 024 7623 4270
Website: www.transport-museum.com
The world's largest collection of British road transport, including 240 cars, commercial vehicles and buses, 100 motorcycles and over 200 cycles.

Brunel's SS *Great Britain*
Great Western Dock, Gas Ferry Road,
Bristol BS1 6TY
Telephone: 0117 927 3416
Website: www.ssgreatbritain.org/Home.aspx
The world's first iron-hulled, screw propeller-driven, steam-powered passenger liner.

Ulster Folk and Transport Museum
153 Bangor Road, Cultra, Holywood
County Down, Northern Ireland BT18 0EU
Telephone: 08448 153139
Website: www.uftm.org.uk
A comprehensive collection demonstrating the history of Irish transport, with a *Titanic* exhibition and an interactive "Flight Experience".

Glossary

Did you read anything you didn't understand?
Some of the more complicated and unusual
terms used in this book are explained here.

amphibious
Able to travel on land or water.

***Apollo* programme**
Costly, but successful, 1960s US
space programme that aimed
to land humans on the Moon.

barge
Long boat used for carrying
freight on rivers and canals and
often towed by another craft.

biofuel
Fuel made from plants, rather
than dug from the ground.

carbon fibre
Very light, strong material used
instead of metal.

emigration
Movement of people to settle
permanently in other countries.

freight
Transport of goods, rather than
passengers, especially by sea.

gridlock
Massive traffic jam that brings
all roads of a city to a halt.

hang-glider
Unpowered aircraft, usually for
a lone pilot, lifted by the wind.

horse power
Unit used to measure the
power of a vehicle's engine, by
comparing it with the pulling
power of a horse.

internal combustion engine
Engine powered by tiny, regular
explosions caused by the
burning of gas or liquid fuel.

jet pack
Jet-powered backpack allowing
someone to fly a short distance.

junk
Chinese ocean-going ship with
a very efficient sail stiffened by
thin strips of wood.

locomotive
The front of a train, holding the
engine, that pulls the carriages.

lunar module
Portion of the *Apollo* spacecraft
that landed on the Moon.

machmeter
Instrument to show how many
times faster than the speed of
sound an aircraft is flying.

mainsail
The biggest sail on a ship.

mariner
Sailor.

metro
Fast city rail transport system,
named after the underground
railways in Paris.

NASA
The National Aeronautics and
Space Administration, the
USA's space agency.

paddle wheel
Large, wide wheel on an early
steamship, used to move the
ship through the water before
the invention of the *propeller*.

production line
Part of a factory where workers
do one task in the manufacture
of a product that moves
continuously along the line.

propeller
Arrangement of several slanting
blades that spin on a ship or
aircraft to power the vehicle.

rocket
A vehicle for launching
spacecraft, with an engine that
can operate without air.

shipwright
Someone who builds ships.

solar panel
Device that captures energy
from the sun, to heat water or
generate electricity.

stagecoach
Horse-drawn coach that ran to
a regular timetable.

steerage class
The cheapest kind of cabin in
a passenger ship from the 19th
and early 20th centuries.

supersonic
Travelling faster than the speed
of sound.

SUV
Sports Utility Vehicle. A large
road car invented to avoid
US government limits on fuel
efficiency and pollution.

Index

Picture credits

The publisher would like to thank the following for their kind permission to reproduce their photographs:

Position key: c=centre; b=bottom; left=left; r=right; t=top

Cover: © David Askham/Alamy

4bc: Pauline Taylor/Alamy; 5tl: Gary Alvis/iStockphoto; 5tr: Images of Africa Photobank/Alamy; 6bc: North Wind Picture Archives/Alamy; 7tr: Adrian Sherratt/Alamy; 7bl: David Morgan/iStockphoto; 8br: Robert Harding World Imagery/Corbis; 9br: iStockphoto; 9cr: iStockphoto; 9tl: US Library of Congress; 10cl: Alexey Dudoladov/iStockphoto; 10cr: iStockphoto; 10bl: iStockphoto; 11bc: Lou Linwei/Alamy; 11tr: Samuel Lemanczyk/iStockphoto; 11cl: Torsen Wittman/iStockphoto; 12tc: iStockphoto; 12bc: National Railway Museum/Science & Society; 13tr: Heritage Image Partnership; 13bl: Holger Mette/iStockphoto; 13tl: iStockphoto; 14bc: iStockphoto; 14tr: iStockphoto; 15bl: Ian Klein/iStockphoto; 15tl: Leonard de Selva/Corbis; 16bc: Science Museum/Science & Society; 17tl: Stefano Bianchetti/Corbis; 18tr: iStockphoto; 18bc: NMeM/Science & Society; 19tr: Bill Philpot/iStockphoto; 19tr: S Greg Panosian/

iStockphoto; 20bc: Gianni Dagi/Corbis; 21cr: Sylvia Cordaiy Photo Library Ltd/Alamy; 22cl: iStockphoto; 22bl: Michel Setboun/Corbis; 23cr: Dane Wirtzfeld/iStockphoto; 23cl: iStockphoto; 23bl: Skysails; 24bc: istockphoto; 24tr: US Library of Congress; 25cl: Mary Evans Picture Library/Alamy; 25tr: US Library of Congress; 26tl: US Library of Congress; 26cl: US Library of Congress; 27tr: Royal Caribbean Cruises Ltd; 27c: Royal Caribbean Cruises Ltd; 27cr: Royal Caribbean Cruises Ltd; 27br: Royal Caribbean Cruises Ltd; 26bl: Mary Evans Picture Library/Onslow Auctions Ltd; 28tl: iStockphoto; 29cr: Bettmann/Corbis; 29tc: MorgueFile; 29tc: MorgueFile; 30bl: US Library of Congress; 30bc: US Library of Congress; 30br: US Library of Congress; 31tc: Heritage Image Partnership; 31br: US Library of Congress; 31bl: US Library of Congress; 32bc: Michael Perris/Alamy; 32tr: NASA; 33cl: Lordprice Collection/Alamy; 34c: Dean Turner/iStockphoto; 34bc: PD-USGOV-Miltary; 35c: A R Pingstone; 35cr: The Print Collector/Alamy; 35tc: Yuri Gripas/Reuters/Corbis; 36tl: NASA; 37bc: NASA; 37tr: NASA; 38br: Peter Titmus/Alamy; 38cr: Rinspeed Inc; 38bl: US Library of Congress; 40tc: NASA; 40bl: Underwood & Underwood/Corbis; 41br: JCB Bamford Excavators Ltd; 41c: Bortal Hajdarevic/iStockphoto; 42tc: Geoffery Holman/iStockphoto; 42bc: HotNYCNews/Alamy; 42bc: iStockphoto; 42tl: Michael Macor/San Francisco Chronicle/Corbis; 43tr: NASA